Nostalgia Doesn't
Flow Away
Like Riverwater

NOSTALGIA DOESN'T FLOW AWAY LIKE RIVERWATER

Xilase qui rié di' sicasi rié nisa guiigu'

La nostalgia no se marcha como el agua de los ríos

POEMS IN DIDXAZÁ
(ISTHMUS ZAPOTEC)
AND SPANISH
BY IRMA PINEDA

ENGLISH TRANSLATIONS
BY WENDY CALL

PHONEME
MEDIA

DEEP
VELLUM

DALLAS, TEXAS

Phoneme Media, an imprint of Deep Vellum Publishing
3000 Commerce St., Dallas, Texas 75226
deepvellum.org · @deepvellum

Deep Vellum is a 501c3 nonprofit literary arts organization founded
in 2013 with the mission to bring the world into conversation through
literature.

Support for this publication has been provided in part by grants from
the National Endowment for the Arts, the Texas Commission on
the Arts, the City of Dallas Office of Arts and Culture's Arts Activate
program, and the Moody Fund for the Arts.

Paperback ISBN: 9781646052783
Ebook ISBN: 9781646052998

LIBRARY OF CONGRESS CONTROL NUMBER: 2023038196

Cover design by Sarah Schulte
Interior layout and typesetting by Andrea García Flores

PRINTED IN CANADA

CONTENTS

Carrying Words Across Borders:
Poetry on/in Migration

In 2008, one of my neighbors in Seattle gave me three of Irma Pineda's poems, hoping I might render them in English. He was a Zapotec immigrant from the Isthmus of Tehuantepec, in southeastern Oaxaca, Mexico; these poems were a voice from his homeland. Entranced by those three poems, written by Pineda in both Spanish and Didxazá (or Isthmus Zapotec), I sent her an email asking if she might be interested in having more of her work translated into English. Not long after that, I received a well-traveled envelope from Juchitán, Oaxaca. Inside, I found four of the five books that Pineda had published at that time (one had already gone out of print).

In the fourteen years since Pineda mailed me those books, I have translated and published in English nearly all of the poems they contain. She has since published eight more books of poetry and I'm continuing to translate my way through her ever-expanding body of exquisite work. We meet in person to discuss every line of every poem I translate. We have presented her poetry in three languages in eight Mexican and U.S. states, interviewed each other for radio shows, organized events for one another's publications, traveled together in both her country and mine, and co-hosted gatherings for Indigenous women writers in southern Mexico.

That border-crossing envelope that I received in 2008 included the first edition of this collection: *Xilase qui rié di' sicasi rié nisa guiigu' / La nostalgia no se marcha como el agua de los ríos*. The book was published in 2007 by Escritores en Lenguas Indígenas, Mexico's national organization of Indigenous-language writers—which would later elect Pineda to serve as its president. She is the only woman ever to have held that position. That book's cover image, in particular, grabbed my attention: a bold red, yellow, and black embroidered huipil, or woman's tunic —called bidaani' in Juchitán. The image is close-cropped to highlight the embroidery; only those familiar with huipils would recognize it as a garment. The design is classic, strongly associated with the Isthmus of Tehuantepec and sometimes used as a symbol of the region. But this specific huipil is part of the British Museum's collection in London. It was carried across the Atlantic Ocean and then its image returned to Mexico, to become a book cover. This powerful symbol refused to remain in a museum collection far from home, insisting on its freedom. This red-and-yellow huipil is a migrant, a border-crossing traveler, one firmly rooted in Binnizá (Isthmus Zapotec) culture and identity. In that way, it represents perfectly the speakers of this book's poems.

My English translations draw on both of Pineda's originals; she publishes most of her work bilingually in Spanish and Didxazá. Pineda refers to the two versions as "mirror poems." Her patient guidance allows me to access the poems in Didxazá, through my understanding of the language is rather basic. In some aspects of grammar and sound, English comes closer to Didxazá than Spanish does, and sometimes I can recreate in English elements of the Didxazá original that Pineda left out of her Spanish version. For example, the sounds we represent in English-language orthography with the letters J and Z don't exist in Spanish, but they do exist in Didxazá. While the use of gender is different in Didxazá and English, it's far more similar than either language is to Spanish.

The thirty-six poems in *Nostalgia Doesn't Flow Away Like Riverwater* are persona poems. They alternate between two fictional voices based in Irma's hometown: someone who has migrated to the United States as an undocumented worker and that migrant's partner, who has stayed behind in Juchitán. Each of the book's three parts includes twelve poems. In Part I, "My Heart in Two," the migrant contemplates the decision to leave, while their spouse anticipates the pain of being left behind. In Part II, "On the Path," twelve untitled poems continue the dialogue between the partners, exploring their separation through place-based metaphor. The dry earth drinks their tears. Nighttime stars transform into the twinkling windows of skyscrapers for the migrant and disappear almost entirely for the person waiting at home, where the town's houses have window-eyes (an image so direct that it's a word-for-word translation from Didxazá) that stare blankly with abandonment. "On the Path" ends with the poem that gives the collection its title. The dozen poems of Part III, "The Day Will Come," carry the two lovers through despair to hope. In the end, the waiting spouse asserts that even if the migrant worker must return empty-handed, having failed to find their fortune in El Norte, their return "will lift our hearts."

Translating this collection into English from the dual poetic traditions of Spanish and Didxazá has meant negotiating a series of border crossings, the process recreating both the literal and figurative stories of this book. These border crossings begin with the title's first word: "nostalgia" in Spanish, "xilase" in Didxazá. "Nostalgia" has similar meanings in English and Spanish, whereas "xilase" is what we would call "melancholia," a physical illness brought on by great trauma or loss. When a person falls ill with xilase, specific treatments must be followed to restore the person's health, or the illness can be fatal. With each line of Pineda's poetry, I could choose either the Spanish or Didxazá path into English. For the book's title, I chose the Spanish path, because of English-language readers' familiarity with the word as well as for its sound and rhythm.

I spent part of my childhood living on the U.S.-Mexico border, in the 1970s when it was far more porous, when there was no wall. There, I learned how words change meaning as they cross borders. Two decades after my family moved away from the border, when I moved to the Isthmus of Tehuantepec, I met many people who had made the border crossing that is explored in this book. The way they referred to their journey to El Norte shocked me. "Me fui de mojado," they would say—"I went as a wetback." In the Isthmus, the word "wetback" was not the terrible slur that I'd known it to be, but rather a mark of distinction. Successfully crossing the deadly U.S. border was a major life accomplishment. It's an experience that irrevocably changes the border-crosser's life: more money, more disconnection, more prestige, more loneliness. The tangled emotions of border-crossing are all bound up in this book. To be wrenched out of one's homeplace is a wound that might heal, but will never disappear. The pull back to the place that holds xquipi', one's ombligo or umbilical cord, interred in your family's land, is lifelong. To leave is not only to miss one's people and one's language, but also the land, flora, fauna, and sea.

During one of our many conversations about the poems in this book, Pineda explained to me, "I create poetry as a way to keep collective memory of my culture alive and to reflect on what is happening to our culture. When I say 'our culture,' of course I'm also referring to the earth, to the sea." The sea is a character in *Nostalgia Doesn't Flow Away Like Riverwater*, triggering the migrant's decision to head north, because, as Pineda writes in Part

II, "the sea stopped birthing fish and now vomits rusted cans." In Part III, "The Day Will Come," the sea reappears, serving as witness and judge of people's decisions as they struggle with the dislocations of climate change and other ecological crises. Part III takes the sea as its central metaphor. Its first poem appears on the page in the form of a marine whirlpool: the word nisado' / mar / sea spirals down the center of the poem, while the rest of the poem whorls around that word like a nautilus shell. (I'd like to give thanks to Fernando Franco, a student in Cecilia Martínez-Gil's literature course at Santa Monica College, whose question about this poem helped me recognize this dynamic.) The nautilus image is centrally important to Indigenous communities throughout Mexico, including the Binnizá. The poem "Sea" forms a spiral in word, shape, and meaning as the sea shifts from being a physical place to a metaphorical place to identity itself when the poem's speaker merges with the sea, personified by it.

The book's longest and most widely circulated poem —in all three languages—is "You Will Not See Me Die." Its refrain, "Qui zuuyu naa gate' / No me verás morir" was inspired by the refrain in a Jaime Sabines poem, "No podrás morir"—"you cannot die." Pineda's poem has been widely circulated in print and digital journals and on social media, adapted into hip hop and dance music versions, inspired YouTube videos, and been quoted on murals in several towns. The English version of "You Will Not See Me Die" has migrated to many places: it has been published three times; there are audio recordings on the websites of two magazines and a half-hour radio documentary about the poem aired on the Australian Broadcasting Corporation's radio series *Earshot*. "You Will Not See Me Die" asserts the survival of the Binnizá and their unbreakable connection to the land that sustains them—even when they must leave it.

Many of the poem's lines reference Isthmus Zapotec fables and stories. For Binnizá readers, each of those lines is a chapter in cultural history. Explaining just one of those stories for the 2017 radio feature I co-produced with Karen Werner, Pineda said: "When I talk about the rabbit and the coyote, that is a very traditional story from this region; it is a story about struggle and resistance. Coyote is a strong character; he's big and ferocious with sharp teeth and claws that can kill. In the story, Coyote is threatening Rabbit—a smaller creature, seemingly defenseless. But Rabbit is very smart and shrewd. He's going to successfully resist and he's always making fun of Coyote and tricking him. Rabbit always escapes and survives. I think this is why we tell this story a lot here. It teaches us that strength alone isn't enough for survival."

The Spanish and Didxazá originals of "You Will Not See Me Die" have been so widely circulated—and are so often requested—that Pineda has retired them from her public readings and performances. She says of the poem, "I gave this child feet and other people are giving it wings. They are giving it meaning that I never would have imagined. It is flying; it doesn't need my voice to be heard anymore. Now, it is heard through other people's voices, with other rhythms . . . In the end, poems are like children, they start to walk on their own."

I am grateful to offer you the poems of *Nostalgia Doesn't Flow Away Like Riverwater* in another rhythm; may they move and walk and fly across many borders.

Wendy Call
Seattle, unceded Duwamish territory
June 2023

I

MY HEART IN TWO

Chupa ladxidua'

Dos mi corazón

YOUR SUITCASE

Pack your suitcase
leave behind all that weighs you down
        that might entangle your feet on the path
You must leave light as a feather
to leap   to fly

Pack your suitcase well
leave the pain here
        I will take good care of it
leave the nostalgia
        so it won't make you sick you once there

But don't forget to take
the gift of the jaguar
        to face the long journey
the gift of the eagle
        so you won't be captured

You must return to your lifeline's home

NI CHINEU'

Guluu chahui' ni chineu' cherica'
bisaana guirá' ni nanaa
        guirá ni guchenda ñeeu lu ca neza ca
Nasisi bia' ti duubi nga cheu'
ti ganda chu'bilu'   ti ganda guipápalu'

Gula'qui' chahui ni chinelu'
bisaana yuuba' cheri'
        naa zanda gapa chahue' laa
bisaana xilase
        qui gunihuará nga lii cherica'

Huaxa si qui gusiaandu' chineu'
xquenda beedxe'
        ti gudxii lulu' ca neza ca
xquenda bisiá
        ti qui gutagunacabe lii

Ra ga'chi' xquipilu' nga guibiguetu'

EL EQUIPAJE

Prepara tu equipaje
deja todo lo que pese
         lo que pueda enredar tus pies en los caminos
Ligero como una pluma debes partir
para saltar   para volar

Prepara bien tu equipaje
deja aquí el dolor
        que yo bien puedo guardarlo
deja la nostalgia
        para que no te enferme allá

Mas no olvides llevar
el don del tigre
        para enfrentar los caminos
el don del águila
        para que ninguna mano te detenga

Al lugar que guarda tu ombligo debes volver

THORN

A thorn deep in my flesh
is pain itself
I want to tear open my skin
to leave it here
> beneath this earth
> that shields the earthen pot
>> house of my birth cord
> the land that holds my lifeline
> the land that will reel me back
so I will return with flowers
> to place on our altar
> and take to my loved ones' graves
But a thorn buried deep
in my flesh is pain

> I will carry this weight with me

TI GUIICHI

Ti guiichi na'zi' ndaani' beela
nga yuuba'
Nuaa guxale' guidubinaca guidilade'
ti gusaanani cheri'
    xha'na' yu di'
    yu ni rudii xidxaa guisu
        ra ga'chi' xquipe'
    layú ni naaze doo xquendanabane'
    layú ni cubayu doo yane'
ti guibigueta' ne guie'
    cuaque' lu mexa bido'
    ne chiniá ra xpa' ca gue'tu' stine'
Xisi ti guiichi daabi dxiichi'
ndaani' beela nga yuuba'

    Ziniá laa neca guinaa

UNA ESPINA

Una espina adentro de la carne
es el dolor
Quiero abrir mi piel entera
para dejarlo aquí
        debajo de esta tierra
        la misma que abriga la olla del barro
            casa de mi ombligo
        la tierra que sostiene el cordel de mi vida
        la que habrá de jalar mis riendas
para volver con flores
        y poner en la mesa de los santos
        y llevar a las tumbas de mis muertos
Pero una espina bien metida
adentro de la carne es el dolor

        Partiré con él aunque me pese

RECOLLECTIONS

Take the sweet recollections that lighten
memory
        children's laughter in village streets
        games played in mud
        grackles' cawing in the afternoon
        the scent of frangipani and isthmus jasmine

Hush that old vulture of nostalgia
stop his cries with the chants
   your mother taught you in Zapotec
tell him the stories your grandfather
   wove in the afternoon

              Speak
                  free your voice

GUENDAREDASILÚ

Yené guendaredasilú naxi ni runi nasisi
guendabiaani'
    xquendaruxidxi xcuidi lu neza guidxi
    guendariguite ndaani' beñe
    ribidxiá sti' bigose huadxí
    xinaxhi guie'chaachi' ne guie'xhuba'

Bindiibi ruaa zo'pe' huela xilase
bisigani ridxi sti' ne riuunda'
    ni bisiidi' jñou' lii didxazá
biui' ne laaca diidxa' ni gudiba
    bixhozegolalu' lu huadxí

                Guní' huaxa
                    bindaa xtiidxalu'

RECUERDOS

Lleva los recuerdos dulces que aligeran
la memoria
       la risa de los niños en las calles del pueblo
       los juegos en el lodo
       el graznido de los zanates en las tardes
       el aroma del *guie'chaachi'* y del *guie'xhuba'*

Amordaza al viejo zopilote de la nostalgia
apaga sus gritos con los cantos
   que en zapoteco te enseñó tu madre
cuéntale las leyendas que tu abuelo
   tejió para la tarde

              Habla
                  suelta tu palabra

THIS SADNESS

I have packed away my belongings
deep in my heart and mind
but what can I do with this sadness
that weighs on us
       Where can I leave it
       so it doesn't become a rope
       hanging from your neck that entangles my feet
I don't want to be the curlew
snared by melancholy
who flew back home
without catching even a glimpse
beyond the clouds

NABANA'

Ndaani' ladxidua' ne ndaani' xquendabiaane'
ma gulaque' chahue' ni chiniá'
nabana' di' nga qui guidxela' xi guneniá laa
nutaguná guiranu
      Qui ganna' xi lu neza gusaana' laa
      ti qui gácani ti doo
      ganda yanilu' ne guirendani ñee'
Qui racaladxe' gaca' dxa berelele
ni gudiidxi xilase laa
ne bigueta' xquidxi
ma qui ñanda ñuuya'
xi nuu deche zá

LA TRISTEZA

En el corazón y en la memoria
he colocado mi equipaje
mas no sé qué hacer con esta tristeza
que nos oprime
    Sobre qué camino podré dejarla
    para que no se convierta en una soga
    colgada de tu cuello y me enrede los pies
No quiero ser el alcaraván
al que abrazó la melancolía
y volvió a su tierra
sin alcanzar a mirar
el otro lado de las nubes

FEAR

Days when it seems
the sun could sear away memory
      scare me
 I fear those on the other side
      who drool honeyed words
      and flit their forked tongues
I fear their words might pierce
your heart

      and change you

DXIIBI

Ruchibi ca dxi ca naa
zándaca gubidxa gucaaguí guendabiaani'
        ne guxiá guendaredasilú
Ridxibe' binni nuu cherica'
        cani rului' nanaxi ruaaca'
        ne rutaabica' ludxica' naduxhu'
Ridxibe' chu' la'dxilu' xtiidxacabe
ne guchou'

                gacalu' stobi

MIEDO

Me asustan los días
puede ser que el sol incendie la memoria
          y borre los recuerdos
Me dan miedo aquellos que están allá
          los que enseñan miel en su boca
          y clavan su filosa lengua
Tengo miedo de que sus palabras entren
en tu corazón

          y te vuelvan otro

US

Our words will carry on as song
        we are children of the trees
who will shade our path
        we are children of the rocks
who will forbid our disappearance

LAANU

Zadundarunu xtiidxanu
      xiiñi yaga nga laanu
laaca' gudiica' bandá' neza ziuunu
      xiiñi guié nga laanu
laaca' gunica' qui gusiaandanu

NOSOTROS

Nuestra palabra seguirá siendo canto
        somos hijos de los árboles
que darán sombra a nuestro camino
        somos hijos de las piedras
que no permitirán el olvido

THIS PATH

The lights twinkling from the river's far side
       dazzle
       dizzy
       deceive

Don't forget why you walk this path
embrace your nahual
       your earthly guardian
Turn your gaze toward home
       where your people stayed
look carefully at your footprints
to remember the path you must retrace

NEZA

Biaani' ni rihuini deche guiigu'
    ruzaani naduxu' bezalú binni
    zanda guché ca' lulu'
    zanda quiteca' lii

Gunna xinga zeu' cherica'
gudiidxi xquendalu'
    ni rapa lii ndaani' guendanabani di'
Bidxigueta lu neza riaana xqui'dxu'
    ra biaana binnili'dxu'
biiya chahui' xtuuba' ñeelu'
ti gannu pa neza guibiguetu'

CAMINO

Las luces que se ven del otro lado del río
      deslumbran la mirada
      marean
      engañan

No olvides tu misión por esos caminos
abraza a tu nahual
      el guardián de tu ser en esta vida
Voltea la mirada hacia tu pueblo
      el lugar donde quedó tu gente
mira bien las huellas de tus pies
para recordar el camino por donde debes volver

TWO PATHS

Our children's sobs
the sadness on my mother's face
        split my heart

If I stay   if I go
I pace in endless circles

If I stay   if I go
both paths lead toward pain

but hunger hurts us, too
                sickness
                poverty's dark night
hurts more

CHUPA NEZA

Xquendaruuna xiiñe'
nabana' lu jñaa
            nganga rindaa ladxidua'

Pa guiaana'   Pa chaa
ricayabie'que' lu ti neza qui zanda guiree cue'

Pa guiaana'   Pa chaa
laaca si ra yuuba' nga zia'

xisi laaca riuuba' guendarindaana
                        guendahuará
                        xquelacahui guendanazi'
jmá runiná

DOS CAMINOS

El llanto de los hijos
la tristeza en el rostro de mi madre
      hace dos mi corazón

Si me quedo   Si me voy
doy vueltas en un camino sin tangente

Si me quedo   Si me voy
son dos senderos que conducen al dolor

pero también nos duele el hambre
      la enfermedad
      la oscura noche de la pobreza
lastima más

IN YOUR HEART

The gift of joy
kept in your heart
will give you good health
will give you the strength to work
will chase away the evil shadows
that surround you

Carry wisdom with you
to illuminate the path under your feet
to remember those in your home
and in your village
still wait for you

NDAANI' LADXIDO'LO'

Guendanayeche' nga gula'qui'
ndaani' ladxido'lo'
ni gudii lii guendanazaaca'
ni gudii lii stipa gudxilulu' dxiiña'
ni guiladxi guirá' bandá' dxaba'
gudiibieque cue'lu'

Guendabiaani' nga yené ra cheu'
ti guzaani neza zé ñeu'
ti qui gusiaandu'
binnili'dxu' ne binnixquidxilu'
cabezaca lii

EN TU CORAZÓN

El don de la alegría
deposita en tu corazón
te dará bienestar
te dará fortaleza para el trabajo
ahuyentará a las malvadas sombras
que ronden tu ser

Inteligencia lleva por donde vas
para alumbrar el camino bajo tus pies
para no olvidar a los que en tu casa
 y en tu pueblo
aún te esperan

DOUBT

Doubt wounds me
not knowing which rocks
      I must stumble over
not knowing which paths lead
      to my destiny
no way to stare
      my future in the face
no longer seeing
      my loved ones' smiles
no way to find
      a heart to hold me
Nowhere feels like home

XIZAA

Runiná xizaa di' naa
qui gunebia'ya' ca guié
      ni chidxelasaa nia'
qui ganna xi neza
      nga chiné naa ra ziaa
qui ganda guuya' guna' nga lu
      ca dxi ni zeeda ca'
ma qui guuya' rua' xquendaruxidxi
      binnilidxe'
qui guidxela' ti ladxido'
      ni quiidxi naa
Ma qui ganna paraa nga lidxe'

DUDA

Me hiere la duda
desconocer las piedras
             con las que habré de tropezar
ignorar los caminos que conducen
             a mi destino
no poder mirar de frente
             el rostro del futuro
no ver más
             la sonrisa de los míos
no encontrar un corazón
             que me de un abrazo
Sentir mi casa en ningún lado

WHEN YOU GO

Leave before daybreak
in the peace of darkness
as sleep still lingers
so tears won't fall before you
so sadness won't hold you back

Go in silence
so when morning blooms
you will be on the path
and the sea of salt we've cried
won't overwhelm you

DXI CHEU'

Guyé laga nuu dxi si bi
laga ca'ru' guirá gueela'
laga nuu xcandaru' binni
ti guiruti' gu'na' neza lulu'
ti qui gucueeza guendanabana' di lii

Dxido' si biree
ne ra guiale' siado' guie'
ma lu neza nga zuhuaalu'
ti qui uganda lii
sidi nisado' ni bi'nadu' di'

CUANDO TE VAYAS

Márchate con la paz del aire
antes de que acabe la noche
mientras el sueño permanece
para que no existan lágrimas frente a ti
para que no te detenga la tristeza

Vete en silencio
cuando florezca la mañana
estarás sobre el camino
y no te alcanzará
la sal del mar que hemos llorado

I WILL RETURN

I leave in the middle of the night
      by the stars' trembling light

I leave you a kiss
and my heart's pain

I carry in my memory
all your smiles
and our shared dreams
of a better future

Weighed down by happiness
in the dawn's frail light
          I will someday return

ZABIGUETA'

Galaa gueela' nga chaa
        ne biaani' racaditi lu ca beleguí

Ti bixidu' ne yuuba' ladxidua'
cusaanania' laatu

Ziniá xa íque'
xquendaruxidxitu'
ne ca bacaanda' ni guninu
chu' dxi nazaaca guibaninu

Ne guendanayeche nuaya'
ne xpiaanihuiini' ti telayú
        ziuu dxi zabigueta'

VOLVERÉ

En medio de la noche me voy
        con la trémula luz de las estrellas

Un beso les dejo
y el dolor de mi corazón

Me llevo en la memoria
sus sonrisas
y los sueños que compartimos
sobre un futuro mejor

Cargado de alegría
con la pequeña luz del alba
            un día volveré

II

ON THE PATH

Lu neza

Sobre el camino

Too long the many sunsets of your absence
and I've found nothing to ease this pain
                    hatcheted in my brain
like a dull blade
            that slowly cleaves my memories
            destroys their scents
            the shadow of your body
that still clings
to the walls of this old house

But my pain's blade
won't kill our hope

Ma ziula nga guca naa ca gubidxa zielu'
ne qui guidxela' ni gusianda yuuba'
                daabi ndaani' íque'
sicasi ñaca ti gudxiu' natuumbu' ruaa
        chaahuidugá cuchuugu' guendaredasilú
            cuxuuxe xinaxhi
            ne bandá' ladilu'
ni cá dxiichi' ru'
cue' yoo yooxho' ralidxinu

Xisi gudxiu' di' qui zaca
yuuba' guuti xquenda ladxidua'

Largos son los soles de tu ausencia
y nada encuentro para remediar este dolor
                    clavado en mi mente
como un cuchillo de boca torpe
          que despacio corta los recuerdos
          destroza sus olores
          la sombra de tu cuerpo
que permanence adherida
a las paredes de la vieja casa

Mas no será el cuchillo
del dolor que nos asesine la esperanza

My feet won't stop
I won't get lost on the path
deep footprints scar the earth's body
countless huaraches rest here
marking the path of those who have passed
my feet won't pause
they both want to make it in time

Qui zabezadxi batañee'
qui zanitedia' lu neza
guete' nexhe' duuba' lu guidiladi layú
stale guelaguidi biaana lu neza
ti gului' ca' pa ladu zé ca ni guzá niru
qui zabezadxi batañee'
ma nuuca' guiuba guedandaca'

No se detendrán mis pies
no me perderé en el camino
profundas son las huellas sobre el cuerpo de la tierra
muchos son los huaraches que reposan
para indicar el sendero de los que se fueron
no se detendrán mis pies
son dos que quieren llegar a tiempo

A drop of salt on paper
is silence killing us
Where have your footsteps taken you?
In what corner of the world
                    do they hear your laughter?
What shard of earth drinks your tears?

Wherever you are
send passenger pigeons
to bring us your voice
Whether or not it arrives here
with the sadness of the rain

Sidi riaba lu gui'chi'
nga dxido' ni cayuti laadu
Paraa yené ñeeu lii
Xi guriá guidxilayú cucaadiaga tuuxa
                   xquendaruxidxilu ya?
Xi ndaa layú di' caye' xquendaruunalu'?

Ratiica nuulu'
biseenda neca ti bere stiá
guedané stiidxalu'
zaa nacati' guedandani rari'
ne nabana' nisaguié

Una gota de sal sobre el papel
es el silencio que nos mata
¿Adónde te han llevado tus pasos?
¿En qué rincón del mundo
                    alguien escucha tu risa?
¿Qué pedazo de esta tierra bebe tus lágrimas?

En cualquier lugar en que te encuentres
envía palomas mensajeras
que nos traigan tu voz
sin importar que llegue aquí
con la tristeza de la lluvia

I set out from the south
left cornfields plowed and parched
one ox thin and one dead
One old boat tied
at the edge of the sea
that was once our glory
but long ago stopped giving us fish
and now vomits rusted cans
that no longer hears our pleas
when we pray
to the fishermen's sacred cross
takes no pity on the fatigue
that clasps our feet
on our processions to the altar
we built for her at the ocean's mouth

The sea went deaf and tossed us
into the desert's arms
The sea went deaf and hurled us
onto someone else's path

Neza guete' biaaxha'
bisaana' ti ñaa ma cá neza nabidxi
ne ti yuze bidxi ne stobi ma guti
Ti balaaga yooxho' bindiibe'
guriá nisado'
ni guca' nandxó'
ni ma xadxi qui rudii laanu benda
ne rudxigueta laanu guiiba' cá tini
ni ma qui rucaa diaga didxa'
ni ruzee ruaanu'
neza lu cru guzebenda
ni qui riá' guendaridxaga
riguiidxi ñeenu
lu neza risaananu pasión ra yu'du'
ni gundisanu ruaa nisado'

Bicuaata diaaga nisado' ne rulaa laanu
lu ca neza bidxi
Bicuata diaaga nisado' ne cuseenda laanu
lu neza gadxé guiidxi

Partí del sur
dejé un campo arado y seco
un buey flaco y uno muerto
Una barcaza vieja atada
a la orilla de la mar
que un día fue nuestra gloria
la que hace tiempo dejó de parir peces
y nos vomita oxidadas latas
la que ya no escucha nuestras plegarias
cuando le rezamos
a la santa cruz de los pescadores
ni se apiada del cansancio que abraza
nuestros pies
en largas procesiones rumbo al templo
que en su honor levantamos en la playa

Ensordeció la mar y nos echa
a los brazos del desierto
Ensordeció la mar y nos arroja
sobre el camino de otros pueblos

Our smile floats away
like the life in this river
"of nutrias" they called it
when the river dogs
played games in it
One day there were so many of us
that the nutrias went away
like our men leave now
like young people leave
Who will have the strength to sustain our roots
if the seeds float away?
To whom will we teach the songs
we inherited from our ancestors?
We will find a hidden branch among the rubble
The rivers can dry up
but the Binnizá will not die

Cayé xquendaruxidxinu
sicasi cayé guendanabani ndaani' guiigu'
"guiigu' bi'cu'" biree lá ni
dxi bi'cu' nisa
gudxite ndaani' ni
Ti dxi gúcanu stale
ne zé ca bi'cu' nisa
sicasi rié yanna ca nguiu
sicasi rié ca badunguiu
Tulaa gudii stipa ti guibani xcú nu ya?
pa ca biidxica cayeca'
Tulaa gusiidinu ca riuunda'
ni bisiidi' binnigula'sa laanu ya?
Ti ná huiini' yaga ga'chi' lade guié zadxelanu
zabidxi nisa guiigu'
xisi qui zati binnizá

Se va nuestra sonrisa
como la vida en este río
"de las nutrias" le llamaron
cuando perros de agua
jugueteaban en él
Un día fuimos tantos
que las nutrias se marcharon
como se van ahora nuestros hombres
como se van los jóvenes
¿Quién dará la fuerza para perpetuar nuestras raíces
si las semillas se van?
¿A quién habremos de enseñar los cantos
que de nuestros abuelos heredamos?
Una rama escondida hallaremos entre las piedras
Se secarán los ríos
más no morirán los binnizá

I traveled the path from the south
my feet blistered with memories
so tired from dragging
all my people's dreams

Are they pushing at my back?
Or am I chasing my own delusion?

Who am I in this madness
in the middle of a sea
           turned to sand?

Neza guete' bedandaya'
cayache bitii lu ñee'
ma bidxagaca' caxubiyú ca'
ni cabeza binni lidxe'

Laacabe nga cucaanacabe deche la?
Pala si xpacaanda sia' nga zinanda ya?

Tu naa ma cayaca íque'
galaa bato' ti nisado'
          málasi guca yuxi

Por el camino del sur he venido
mis pies explotan sus recuerdos ampulosos
cansados están de llevar a rastras
las esperanzas de los míos

¿Son ellos los que me empujan las espaldas
o es mi propia quimera la que persigo?

¿Quién soy en esta delirante hora
en medio de un mar
       que se volvió arena?

The houses of your village have eyes
that seek the beach's sandgrains
in the distance they see the sun
that doesn't shine on their heads today
doesn't brighten their shingle-tresses
painted black, red and soft colors
Who lives under the pink or yellow roofs?
Who is in the dark houses?

Winding toward the mountains the only
visible artery of your village's body disappears
perhaps because
it's the path that leads to the sea
gloomy village
showing only one mouth-door
painted red

Where did its lifeblood go?
Did its unbearable silence scare away
the dogs?
There are no children in the street,
not even robbers prowling the roofs
Even the birds have gone away...

Ca yoo xquidxilu' napaca' lu
cuyubica yuxi nisado'
cayuyadxica' gubidxa
cadi cuzaani íqueca'
cadi cutiee guichaíque dexa ca'
dié nayaase, naxiñá ne na té
Tuunga nabeza xa'na' íque yoo na té ne naguchi ca
ya?
Tulaa ndaani' ca yoo nacahui ca?

Neza ca dani riniti
tobiluchasi neza rihuiini ndaani' guidxi
tisi ndi nga ni ribee binni
ruaa nisado'
Guidxi nacahuigá
ni cului'si ti ruaa
dié naxiñá

Paraa zé xrinibe?
Xquendadxido'be nga bichibi
bi'cu' la?
Qui guinni xcuidi lu guidxi
ni gubaana qui richesabi íque yoo
Ca manihuiinica laaca zié ca'…

Las casas de tu pueblo tienen ojos
que buscan arenas de la playa
ven a lo lejos el sol
que hoy no brilla sobre sus cabezas
no ilumina sus cabellos-tejas
pintadas de negro, rojo y suaves colores
¿Quién habita bajo los techos rosas o amarillos?
¿Quién en las casas obscuras?

Rumbo a las montañas se pierde
la única arteria visible del cuerpo de tu pueblo
acaso porque ésta sea
el camino que lleva al mar
Pueblo sombrío
que sólo enseña una boca-puerta
pintada de rojo

¿Adónde fue su sangre?
¿fue su insoportable silencio
el que asustó a los perros?
No hay niños en la calle,
ni siquiera ladrones brincando por los techos
Las aves también se marcharon…

Many full moons have passed
since I yanked my feet
from southern lands
The iron horse didn't rush its pace
and left us time
to remember

I don't know which hurts us more
the misfortunes we left behind
or those we find here
becoming invisible
no one looks into my black eyes
no one hears the songs on my tongue
is my brown skin transparent?

Ma stale beeu' gudi'di'
de dxi guxha' ñee'
ndaani' layú guete'
Qui ñacapurá mani' guiiba'
ne bidiisi laadu
jmaru' guendaredasilu'

Qui ganna dia' xi jmá naná
pa ni bisaanadu cherica'
pa ni cadxeladu cheri'
ra qui rihuinidu'
guiruti' ruyadxi nayaase bezalua'
guiruti' rucaa diaga riuunda riale ndaani' rua'
zandaca rididibiaani lu guidilade' nayasegá

Muchas lunas han girado
desde que arranqué los pies
de las tierras del sur
No aceleró el tren sus pasos de hierro
y nos dejó tiempo
para la memoria

No sé si nos duelen más
las desgracias que allá dejamos
o las que encontramos aquí
vueltos invisibles seres
nadie mira mis oscuros ojos
nadie escucha el canto que brota de mi lengua
¿es acaso transparente mi piel morena?

Since you left
our sliver of sky
is starless but sometimes
one star gleams and becomes
more brilliant as I watch
and I think maybe it's the same
sliver you see over there

De dxi zieu'
ti ndaa guidxilayú di'
qui gapa beleguí
nuu tiru ribee lu tobi
pa guyadxié laa rutuxu xpiaani'
ne rabe' zandaca cherica'
ngueca beleguí cayuuyalu' lii

Desde tu partida
esta parte del cielo
está vacía de estrellas
de vez en cuando asoma una
si la miro parece brillar más
y pienso que tal vez allá
es la misma que tu miras

The sky rains endless stars on me
they aren't lightning bugs that dance
nor God's eyes watching me
for a long time their saints
have only shown us their eyelids
but I lift my gaze and the sky
rains down endless stars
        ferocious lights in metal towers

Cundaa guibá' stale beleguí luguia'ya'
cadi bacuzaguí cuyaa nga laaca'
cadi bezalu diuxi cayuyadxi naa
ma xadxi nga xpido'be
nisi guidilagaca' rului'ca'
xisi rindizalua' guibá'
ne rului' cayaba stale beleguí
        biaani' duxu' ndaani' ca yoo ro' guiiba ca' nga

Me llueve el cielo su infinidad de estrellas
no son luciérnagas que danzan
ni son los ojos de dios los que me miran
hace tiempo que sus santos
sólo nos muestran la piel de sus párpados
pero alzo la vista y el cielo
me llueve su infinidad de estrellas
       son feroces luces en las torres de metal

I hear the city's roar
its turmoil sharpens my wish
to know its viscera
to tread its ashen skin

I walk brushing the wall
and try to catch the scent
of wet earth
but the grayed asphalt
slaps me away

Rucaadiaga' cabidxiaa guidxiro'
ridxagayaa pabia' riniibi
ne xiñee nga nuaa gunebia'ya' laa
zaya' lu guidiladi na té

Cazaya' ne caxubenaya' cue' yoo
nuaa chu' xie' xinaxhi
yu dxe'
xisi lu té guidxiro' di'
rigapa dxe' rua'

Oigo el rugir de la ciudad
su agitación azora mi insistencia
de conocer sus entrañas
de recorrer su piel gris

Camino rozando la pared
intento percibir el aroma
a tierra húmeda
más el asfalto grisáceo
abofetea mi intención

Nostalgia doesn't melt like water underfoot
it won't climb on a horse
to be carried far from our hearts
It stays here
anchored
rooted in racked flesh
drinking up our tears
and roiling our blood

Nostalgia doesn't flow away
like riverwater
but becomes a sea
that pulls at us relentlessly

Xilase qui raca nisa xa ñee binni
qui rigui'ba' deche mani'
ni nuxale' laa ladxido'
Riaana rari'
naaze dxiichi'
gui'di' lu beela naná
caye' nisa ruuna binni
ne rusiayasi rini

Xilase qui rié di'
sicasi rié nisa guiigu'
laa raca ti nisado'
qui ria' rixubiyú laanu

La nostalgia no se hace agua bajo los pies
no se sube al lomo de ningún caballo
que la lleve lejos del corazón
Se queda aquí
aferrada
asida a la doliente carne
se bebe las lágrimas
y nos alborota la sangre

La nostalgia no se marcha
como el agua de los ríos
se vuelve un mar
que nos arrastra implacable

III

THE DAY WILL COME

Zedandá ti dxi

Un día llegará

SEA

My heart is a sea
where countless fish play
        exultant fish in nostalgia's salt

Absence pains me
distance wounds me
but light shines in this sea
        this sea learned to sense
                others' hearts
        this sea knows to look
                deep into eyes
        this sea learned
                to quiet its powerful waves
                to control the tide
to go unnoticed, to go unseen
because it now knows
not everyone loves the sea

TI NISADO'

Ti nisado' nga ladxidua'
benda ni que rati caguite rari'
      benda nayeche' ndaani' sidi sti' xilase

Riuuba naa qui guinne racá
runiná neza zitu di' naa
xisi nuu biaani' ndaani' nisado' di'
      bisiidi' nisado' di' naa
            xi nuu ndaani' ladxido' sti binni
      nanna nisado' di' guyadxí
          ndaani' bezalú
      bisiidi' nisado' di'
          gusigani nisa ni riabantaa ruaa
          nanna gucueeza nisa ni rigui'ba'
ti qui gannacabe pa nuu, ti qui guihuinni
ti ma nanna yanna
cadi guirá tu nadxii nisado'

UN MAR

Un mar es mi corazón
infinitos peces juegan en él
        peces alegría en la sal de la nostalgia

Me duele la ausencia
me lastima la distancia
pero hay luz en este mar
        aprendió este mar a sentir
                el corazón de los otros
        sabe este mar mirar
                adentro de los ojos
        aprendió este mar
                a callar sus intensas olas
                a controlar la marea
para que no se note, para que no se vea
porque sabe ahora
que no todos aman el mar

LIKE A FLOWER

A cold wind whips my heart
some   who came with me
          will not return

All they dreamed
was lashed by thirst
along the parched path

I couldn't hold their hands
I couldn't drag their feet
      and help them move a bit farther
      on the path to home
To arrive at their family's tomb
      and not just die strangers
      where no one knew their names

What can I do now
but cry as I remember them
      and remember those awaiting
      their return with joy
      they planted in the earth

What can I say to their people
What can I do so these deaths
don't hurt

If only my tears could serve
to water fields
and coax new life
to bloom

SICA TI GUIE'

Ti bi nanda caguiñe ladxidua'
ca xpine'   ca ni bedaniá'
                 ma qui zabiguetaca'

Guirá ni guni' xcaandacabe
guendariatinisa gudiñentaa laaca'
lu ca neza bidxi ca

Qui ñanda ninaaze' nácabe
qui ñanda nixubeyua' ñeecabe
        ti nizarucabe neca sti ndaa neza
        ni nudxigueta' laacabe xquidxinu
ti niguiabacabe ra xpa' binnilidxicabe
        ne qui ñaanacabe sica ti dxu ni biaba
ratiicasi
        guiruti' ñanna tu la'

Xiru ndi gune' ya'
nisi guuna' ra guini' íque laacabe
        ne xpinnicabe ni cabeza
        guibiguetacabe ne guendanayeche'
        ti gudxibacabe laa ra ñaa

Xindi guinié neza lu ca binni ca yanna
xi zanda gune' ti qui guiuuba' laacabe
ca gue'tu' di ya

Neca nisa ni ruuna' di' niquiiñe
ti nuguu gudxa layú
ti ñanda lu sti bieque
sica ti guie' guendanabani ñaleru'

COMO UNA FLOR

Un helado viento golpea mi corazón
aquellos   con los que vine
                    no volverán

Todos sus sueños
fueron azotados por la sed
sobre los áridos caminos

No pude sostener sus manos
no pude arrastrar sus pies
          y hacerlos avanzar un poco más
          hacia el camino de nuestro pueblo
Para llegar a la tumba de sus muertos
          y no caer en cualquier sitio como extraños
          de los que nadie supo el nombre

Pero qué puedo hacer ahora
más que llorar al recordarlos
          y recordar a quienes esperan
          que ellos vuelvan con la alegría
          que habrían de sembrar en la tierra

Qué puedo decir frente a los suyos
qué puedo hacer para que no duelan
estos muertos

Si al menos mis lágrimas sirvieran
para humedecer los campos
y hacer que de nuevo
como una flor se abra la vida

I am now a desert
all the water that traveled my body
has poured over you

My eyes are dry
how much more can I cry
knowing well
that I won't live long enough
to suffocate the sadness
that clutches us

Naa naca yanna ti neza bidxi
guirá nisa ni biuu lade ma bindaate' laa
luguialu'

Nabidxizé ma nuu bezalua'
xiru ndi zanda guuna'
pa nannaca'
qui zugaanda ca dxi xquendanabane'
ti guutexie' nabana'
ni nutaguna' laadu yanna

Yo soy ahora un desierto
toda el agua que habitó mi cuerpo
sobre ti la he derramado

Secos están mis ojos
cuánto más puedo llorar
si bien sé
que no alcanzarán los días de mi vida
para asfixiar la tristeza
que en sus manos nos oprime

Cry no more for your dead
            who now rest underground
save your tears for the children
            who are still lost
They wandered off the path
I feel their home underfoot
but their hearts are no longer
rooted among us

Ma cadi gu'nalu' runi cani ma guti
      laaca' ma nexedxica xa'na yu
gupa xquendaruunalu ti nuuru xiinu
      cananiti ndaani' guidxilayú
Cadi lu neza di' biaanaca'
nanna dxiiche' paraa nabezaca'
xisi ndaani' xquidxinu
ma guxhaca' xcú ladxido'ca'

No llores más por tus muertos
   que bajo la tierra ya descansan
guarda lágrimas para los hijos
   que aún perdidos están
No quedaron en el camino
bien conozco su habitación
pero entre nosotros no está más
la raíz de su corazón

WHO ARE WE

Who are we
      all of us
      who seem different now
Where is our home
where have our songs gone
the magpies' raucous calls so far away
the joyful flowers illuminating
      my mother's huipils forgotten
my children won't hear the stories
      born in my father's mouth
my childhood days stay silent
      before the shame of being different
we hear only the city's rumble
      the rusted days
We have forgotten the name
that gave us life
      that shadow I wanted to erase
Who are we now
all of us
who once wanted to be like the others?

TU LAADU

Tu laadu
  Laadu
  yanna ma gadxé si laadu
Paraa biaana lidxidu
paraa zé riuunda stidu
ma zitu nga biaana ridxi yaya sti' xahui
ma biaanda guendanayeche' sti' ca guie'
  ni ruzaani' lu xtaani' jñaa
ca xiiñe' ma qui zucaadiagaca' diidxa'
  ni biele' ndaani' ruaa bixhoze'
ma bigani ca dxi guca' xcuidi
  rutuiluca' naa nuaa gaca' stobi
nisi ridxi raca ndaani' ti guidxi ro' nga riudiaga'
  ne tini sti' ca dxi ca
Bisiaandadu xa lá
ni bisibani laanu
  nácani yanna ti bandá' nuaa guxiaya'
Tu laadu yanna
laadu
cani gucala'dxinu stobi nga ñacadu?

QUIÉNES SOMOS

Quiénes somos
      nosotros
        los que ahora parecemos otros
Dónde quedó nuestra casa
adónde se han marchado nuestros cantos
lejos quedaron los alborotados gritos de la urraca
en el olvido está la alegría de las flores
        que iluminan los huipiles de mi madre
mis hijos no escucharán las historias
        que nacieron de la boca de mi padre
los días de mi infancia guardan silencio
        frente a la vergüenza de sentirme otro
no se oye más que el rumor de la ciudad
        los días oxidados
Hemos olvidado el nombre
que nos dio origen
        esa sombra que borrar quisiera
¿Quiénes somos ahora
nosotros
los que un día quisimos ser como los otros?

YOU WILL NOT SEE ME DIE

You will not see me die
        you won't forget me
I am your mother
your father
your grandfather's old stories
our age-old traditions
the tear welling from an ancient willow
the saddest branch
        lost among the leaves
You will not see me die
because I am
a reed-woven basket
        where the old spiny lobster
        still waves his pincers
the fish eaten by God
the snake that gulped down a rabbit
the rabbit that always teased the coyote
the coyote that swallowed a wasps' nest
the honey that wells from my breasts
I am your lifeline
        and you will not see me die
You may think everyone has gone away but
you will not see me die
There will be a seed
        hidden in the scrub by the path
that must return to this land

and seed the future
and feed our souls
and our stories will be reborn
and you will not see me die
because we will stay strong
we will always survive
our song will live forever
we will be ourselves and you
and our children's children
and the earth's quaking
        that will shake the sea
and we will be many hearts
        anchored to the core of the Binnizá
and you will not see me die
        you will never see me die
                you will never see
                        me die

QUI ZUUYU NAA GATE'

Qui zuuyu naa gate'
          qui zanda gusiaandu' naa
Naa nga jñou'
bixhozelu'
diixa' yooxho' bixhozególalu
guirá ni ma bisiaa ca dxi ca lii
nisa ruuna ti guesa ma stale dxi bibani
ti na' yaga ni jmá nabana'
          biniti lade bandaga
Quí zuuyu naa gate'
ti naa nga
ti dxumi zu
          ra caniibi ru' na'
          bixhoze bendabuaa
benda ni gudó diuxi
beenda ni bichá ruaa ti lexu
lexu ni gudxite gueu'
gueu' ni gubi lidxi bizu
dxiña bizu ni rindani lu xhidxe'
xquipilu' nga naa
          ne qui zuuyu gate'
Neca zacuxhou' má guirá tu zé
qui zuuyu naa gate'
ziuu ti xhuba'
          ga'chi' lade gui'xhi' nuu lu neza
ndaani' guidxi di' zabigueta'

ne laa gusindani guendanabani
ne laa gaca' gueta xquendanu
ne laa gusibani stiidxanu
ne qui zuuyu naa gate'
ti zácanu nadipa'
ti zabáninu xhadxí
ti riuunda stinu qui zati
ti zácanu laanu ne lii
ne ca xiiñi xiiñinu
ne xú guidxilayú
      ni guniibidxacha nisadó
ne zácanu stale ladxidó'
      naaze dxiichi xquenda binnizá
ne qui zuuyu gate'
      qui zuuyu naa gate'
            qui zuuyudiou'
                  naa gate'

NO ME VERÁS MORIR

No me verás morir
        no podrás olvidarme
Soy tu madre
tu padre
la vieja palabra de tu abuelo
la costumbre de los tiempos
la lágrima que brota de un anciano sauce
la más triste de las ramas
        perdida entre las hojas
No me verás morir
porque soy
un cesto de carrizo
        donde aún se mueven las tenazas
        del papá del camarón
el pescado que Dios comió
la serpiente que devoró un conejo
el conejo que siempre se burló del coyote
el coyote que tragó un panal de avispas
la miel que brota de mis senos
tu ombligo soy
        y no me verás morir
Aunque creas que todos se han marchado
no me verás morir
Habrá una semilla
        escondida entre los matorrales del camino
que a esta tierra ha de volver

y sembrará el futuro
y será alimento de nuestras almas
y renacerá nuestra palabra
y no me verás morir
porque seremos fuertes
porque seremos siempre vivos
porque nuestro canto será eterno
porque seremos nosotros y tú
y los hijos de nuestros hijos
y el temblor de la tierra
   que sacudirá el mar
y seremos muchos corazones
   aferrados a la esencia de los binnizá
y no me verás morir
   no me verás morir
     no me verás
       morir

SOWING

I wanted to sow
the day's sweat in distant lands
it wasn't corn that sprang up
but metal that shackles
our hearts

How can we return to our land
if nostalgia has killed it
not a drop of honey left in its belly
to sweeten our homeplace

Only salt awaits me
from the sea that watches us
with bitter eyes
with the salt from its eyes
the salt from your eyes
that has furrowed the earth
with so much loss
your children's eyes
your father's eyes
your brothers' eyes

Eyes that could wait no longer
eyes so tired of searching
for a ray of sunlight
eyes lost in the underground

path that carries them each day
toward the metal that moves them
to make other machines
invisible as they give up their lives

Now we will sow in the earth
machines that will banish
happiness
from the eyes of those who await them

NI CUDXI'BADU

Ne nisaluna sti' ca dxi ca
gucaladxe' nudxiiba' biní ndaani' guidxi zitu
cadi xuba' di' bindani
gule guiiba' ni nadipa'
nundiibi ladxidua' ne ca xpinne'

Xi ñaca ti nibigueta' xquídxinu
pa xilase ma biiti laa
ma gasti' ndaani' cadxi dxiñayaaga
nusinaxhi guendaribeza di'

Ma gasti' ru' nuu nisi sidi
sti' nisado' cayuyadxi laanu
naguundu bezalú
ne sidi bezalú
ne sidi bezalulu'
ni ma gundaa layú
ne guendaribana
lu ca xiiñu'
lu bixhozelu'
lu ca biza'nalu'

Bezalú ra ma qui ñanda nudxi'banu dxi
bezalú ni ma bidxaga cuyubi
neza ra riree xpiaani' gubidxa
bezalú ni cananiti xhanayú

lu neza ni riné laaca
ra nuu guiiba' runiibi laaca
ti gunica' jmá guiiba'
ni gudii guendanabani ra guiruti' cayuuya'

Xhanayú nga rudxi'badu yanna
guiiba' ni gunduuxe
guendanayeche'
nuu lu binni ni cabeza xpinni

LA SIEMBRA

Con el sudor de los días
quise sembrar en nuevas tierras
no fue maíz lo que brotó
sino metales que con fuerza
atan mi corazón y el de los míos

Cómo volver a la tierra nuestra
si la nostalgia la ha matado
no queda en su vientre una gota de miel
para endulzar las esperanzas

No me espera más que la sal
del mar que nos mira
con resentidos ojos
con la sal de sus ojos
la sal de tus ojos
que han hecho surcos en la tierra
de tanto extrañar
los ojos de tus hijos
los ojos de tu padre
los ojos de tus hermanos

Ojos en los que no pudimos sembrar más días
ojos que casados están ya de buscar
por donde sale la luz del sol
ojos perdidos en el subterráneo

del camino que los lleva cada día
rumbo al metal que los mueve
para crear otras máquinas
que den vida donde nadie los ve

Sembramos ahora bajo la tierra
máquinas que habrán de terminar
con la alegría
en los ojos de quienes esperan

The days won't end
it won't be death arriving with your eyes
it won't be the metal you planted in distant lands
that holds your body
    You will return to me
lugging your heavy bags
in clothes woven of pain
and words carried from the other side
You will return with strange rhythms
unrecognizable thoughts
I won't hold fear in my hands
but rather my heart's song

Qui zaluxe ca dxi ca
cadi guendaguti nga guedané bezalulu'
cadi guiiba' ni bidxiibalu' ndaani' guidxi zitu
nga quiidxi ladilu'
       Zeedu ra nuaa
neca nanaa ni nualu'
neca neu' ti lari yuuba'
ne ca diidxa' ni biziidilu' checá
Zedaneu' gadxé saa
guendabiaani' ni qui zacabia'du'
xisi cadi dxiibi zadxe'lu' ndaani' naya'
riuunda ladxidua' nga guicou'

No se acabarán los días
no será la muerte la que venga con tus ojos
no será el metal que sembraste en lejanas tierras
quien abrace tu cuerpo
       Vendrás a mí
cargando tu pesado equipaje
tu manto hecho de penas
y las palabras que de allá tomaste
Vendrás con extraños ritmos
pensamientos que no habremos de reconocer
mas no habrá entre mis manos miedo
sino el canto del corazón

I clawed a path underground with my fingernails
         no light, no air
The only thing that kept me alive
was the hope of finding you
like a divine queen
waiting for me at tunnel's end
Your shadow my breath, the light
illuminating all the paths I traveled
seeking
a hand to lift me
a heart to shelter me
a mouth to smile at my words
like the laughter of my children
who stayed behind
who wait for me
so that I might return
         with blessed wonder

Ne bixuganaya' gudaañe' ti neza xhanayú
        qui gapa biaani', qui gapa bi
Ni bidii guendanabani naa cherica' nga
nisi cabeza' guidxaaga' lii
rixui'lua' lii sica ti xunaxi do'
rua neza que zuhuaalu' cabezu' naa
Banda' stiu' que nga guca bi, guca biaani'
ni bizaani' guirá neza guzaya'
canayube'
ti ná nindisa naa
ti ladxidó' nudii xidxaa
ti ruaa nuxidxiné ruaa
sicasi ruxidxi ca xiiñe huiine'
ca ni biaana
cani cabeza naa
guedaniá
        guendaridxagayaa

Con las uñas cavé un camino bajo la tierra
          un camino sin luz, sin aire
Sólo me dio vida la esperanza
de encontrarme contigo
como una princesa sagrada
que me esperaba al final del túnel
Tu sombra fue mi aire, la luz
que iluminó todos los caminos que recorrí
en busca
de una mano que me levantara
de un corazón que me diera abrigo
de una boca que sonriera frente a mi boca
como si fuera la risa de mis hijos
los que quedaron
los que me esperan
para que vuelva
          con el asombro

So many times the earth has turned
So many times the moon has bled light
and you have not come back
You wrote it down
you sent your word
saying you'll return soon
Every day   every night
I wait
for your knock at the door
to see the joy on your face
to hear you say
"I've come back
with all I walked that path to find
we'll want for nothing
our bond won't ever be broken"
            I hope for that
                        I wait for you

Panda bieque ma bidii guidxilayú di'
panda beeu' ma bixhii rini biaani' sti'
ne lii qui ganda guibiquetu'
Bicou' guichi'
biseendu diidxa'
ná lu' ma yaca guedandou'
Guirá si dxi   guirasi gueela'
naa cabeza'
guxidxinalu lu yaga ruaa yoo
ne guuya' guendanayeche' lulu'
ne gabilu' naa
"ma bibigueta
niá ni yecaa cherica'
ma gasti' ziaadxa laanu
ma qui ziu dxi guilaa xquendalisaanu"
              Nga nga cabeza'
                      lii nga ribeza'

Cuántas veces ha girado el mundo
cuántas lunas han derramado su iluminada sangre
y tú no has vuelto
Escribiste sobre el papel
palabras enviaste
dices que ya pronto volverás
Cada día   cada noche
yo espero
que tus manos toquen sobre la madera de la puerta
para contemplar la alegría en tu rostro
y escuchar que dices
"he vuelto
he traído lo que fui a buscar por otros caminos
nada nos faltará
no volverá a deshacerse esta unión"
          Eso espero
                    te espero

I know where I come from
I know someone awaits me
it's the cord binding me to my nahual
it's the lamp lighting the path home
But I will not return whole
in these distant lands
half my heart remains
I was one person before uprooting myself
another I learned to be here
Now with a divided heart
How can I keep it from breaking?
If I stay
I will miss my people and my soul
If I go back
it will hurt to hold in my hands
all that I discovered here
How can I keep my heart whole?

Nanna' paraa biree
nanna' nuu tu cabeza naa
ngá nga doo ni bindiibi guenda rizayania'
ngá nga biaani' ni guzaani neza ra guibigueta'
Xisi ma cadi guiza' di nga ziaa
ndaani' ca guidxi zitu di' cayaana
ti galaa ladxidua'
Tobi nga naa dxi guxha ñee' ndaani' xquidxe'
stobi nga biziide' gaca'cheri'
Chupa nga naca yanna ladxidua'
Xi zanda gune' ti qui nilaani zacá?
Pa guiaana cheri'
xpinne' ne xquenda' zabana'
Pa guibigueta cherica'
guirá ni bidxagalua' rari'
rului' cagubayuca' naya'
Xi zanda gune' ti qui nilaa ladxidua' zacá?

Conozco mi origen
sé que alguien me espera
es la cuerda que ata al nahual que me acompaña
es la luz que alumbrará el camino para volver
Mas no volveré del todo
en estas lejanas tierras queda
la mitad de mi corazón
Uno era cuando arranqué los pies de allá
otro aprendí a ser por acá
Dos es ahora mi corazón
¿Qué puedo hacer para no se divida?
Si me quedo
a los míos y mi esencia extrañaré
Si vuelvo allá
las cosas que aquí encontré
en las manos me dolerán
¿Qué puedo hacer para que no sea dos mi corazón?

The day will come
when I can gaze at your face
although it will be only part of you
that returns to us
it won't matter if you return empty-handed
we will embrace you
and your presence will lift our hearts
I hope the day will come
when we will see only green fields
and the nutrias playing in the river
and the fish leaping at the delta
I insist
           that day will come...

Zedandá ti dxi
ra ganda guuya' lulu'
neca ti ndaa si lii
guibigueta ndaani' guidxi di'
neca gasti' naaze nou' guiuulu'
zaguiidxidu lii
ne zieche ladxido'do ti ma nuulu'
Cabeza' guedandá ti dxi
nisi naga' guuya' ca ñaa nuu cheri'
ne caguite bi'cu' nisa ndaani' guiigu'
ne cachesa benda ruaa nisado'
Naa rabe
        zedandá ti dxi...

Llegará el día
en que pueda contemplar tu rostro
aunque sólo una parte de ti sea
la que vuelva con nosotros
no importará que vuelvas con las manos vacías
te abrazaremos
y nuestro corazón se alegrará por tu presencia
Espero que llegue el día
en que sólo verdor miremos en los campos
y los juegos de las nutrias en el río
y el salto de los peces en la boca del mar
yo digo
       que llegará un día…

Acknowledgments

The translation into English of this poetry collection was made possible by a 2015 Literature Fellowship in Translation from the National Endowment for the Arts (NEA), a federal agency. Both translator and poet are enormously grateful for this support and for the kindness of the NEA staff.

Warm thanks to the following publications, where the English translations of many of the poems in *Nostalgia Doesn't Flow Away Like Riverwater* first appeared—sometimes in slightly different versions and in many cases alongside their Didxazá and Spanish originals. Gratitude to the journal editors whose comments improved the English translations.

"Your Suitcase"; the first, third, fifth, and twelfth poems in the "On the Path" series; "[Cry no more for your dead]"; and "You Will Not See Me Die" appeared in *Michigan Quarterly Review* (Fall 2013).

"Thorn" and "Sowing" appeared in *Diálogo* (Spring 2016).

"Recollections," "This Sadness," and "Fear" appeared in *North Dakota Quarterly* (Fall 2020).

"This Path," "Two Paths," "Doubt," "I Will Return,"

and the eighth, tenth, and eleventh poems from "On the Path" appeared in *NAIS (Native American and Indigenous Studies) Journal* (Fall 2020).

"When You Go" appeared in *Poet Lore* (Fall 2019).

The second and sixth poems from "On the Path" appeared in *Shenandoah* (Spring 2020).

The fourth poem from "On the Path" and "Who Are We" appeared in *Cincinnati Review* (Winter 2016).

The seventh poem in "On the Path" appeared in *SAND Journal* (Spring 2015).

"Sea" appeared in *About Place* (Summer 2016).

"You Will Not See Me Die" appeared in *World Literature Today* online (Winter 2012) and on the websites of the National Endowment for the Arts and Mary's Pence Foundation.

"Like a Flower" appeared in *Kenyon Review Online* (October 2020).

"[The days won't end]," "[I know where I come from]," and "[The day will come]" appeared in *Origins* (Spring 2016).

Many thanks to the Jack Straw Cultural Center, Ragdale Foundation, and Seattle CityArtist Program for their support of the translation of these poems. The Helen Riaboff Whiteley Center of the University of Washington and our friend David Palmer made possible direct collaboration between poet and translator. Much gratitude to Adela Ramos and Sejal Shah, and especially Shook— editor extraordinaire at Phoneme—for their thoughtful and extremely helpful feedback on the English translations. All praise to Deep Vellum and the National Endowment for the Arts for believing in this book.

Irma Pineda is the author of ten books of bilingual Didxazá/Spanish poetry and two volumes of poetry in Spanish. She is also the translator of several Didxazá/Spanish books and a collaborator or co-editor of several anthologies. Her poems have been translated into ten languages and published throughout Europe and the Americas. Her 2018 collection, *Naxiña' Rului' ladxe' – Rojo Deseo*, won Mexico's Caballo Verde Prize, awarded for the year's best book of poetry. Together with Wendy Call, she won the 2022 John Frederick Nims Memorial Prize for Translation, awarded by the Poetry Foundation. Pineda is a professor of intercultural education at the Ixtepec, Oaxaca, campus of Mexico's Universidad Pedagógica Nacional. Between 2018 and 2021 she served as a senior advisor for education, cultural issues, and science for the Mexican Federal Legislature. From 2020 through 2022 she served as Vice President of the United Nations Permanent Forum on Indigenous Issues, one of two representatives for all the Indigenous peoples of Latin America. She lives in her hometown of Juchitán, Oaxaca.

Wendy Call translated Irma Pineda's *In the Belly of Night and Other Poems*, published in 2022 by Pluralia/Eulalia, and wrote the award-winning nonfiction book *No Word for Welcome: The Mexican Village Faces the Global Economy* (Nebraska, 2011). She has co-edited two anthologies: *Telling True Stories: A Nonfiction Writers' Guide* (Penguin, 2007) and *Best Literary Translations* (Deep Vellum, 2024). Her translations of poetry by Indigenous Latin American women have been supported by the Fulbright Commission, Institute for Comparative Modernities at Cornell University, and National Endowment for the Arts. Call teaches creative nonfiction in Pacific Lutheran University's MFA program. She lives in southeast Seattle, on Duwamish land, and in Oaxaca City, on Mixtec and Zapotec land.